THE GROW GIVER'S GUIDE TO MULTI-FAMILY REAL ESTATE INVESTING FOR BEGINNERS

By Justin Hoke

Dedication

This book is dedicated to Pace Morby, Veena Jetti, Carlos Salguero, Keston Glasgow, Karolyn & Miron Briley, Ryan Kocherhans, The CondorMFH Team, Yatang Hoke, Julie Burkhardt and the entire SUBTO Community for their guidance, support, and encouragement in my journey in multi-family real estate investing. Their wisdom and experience have inspired me to share this knowledge with others.

Additionally, I would like to express my gratitude to ChatGPT, the advanced language model that helped put these ideas into a readable format. The technology provided by OpenAI has been a valuable tool in the creation of this book.

Without the help and support of these individuals and the assistance of ChatGPT, this book would not have been possible. Thank you for everything.

TABLE OF CONTENTS:

Hello everyone, my name is Justin Hoke and I am the founder of the Grow Giver Community and podcast as well as a founding member of Condor Multifamily Housing Solutions. I am thrilled to be writing this book and sharing my experiences with you all. Our team has been working in the multi-family housing industry for a short period of time and while I am still fairly new myself, I am passionate about helping others navigate this complex and ever-evolving market.

Recently, my team and I had the opportunity to go under contract on a 14 million dollar deal in Corpus Cristi, Texas. Although the deal did not end up closing, we learned valuable lessons along the way that have shaped our understanding of the multi-family housing industry and informed the content of this book. Despite incurring costs of around 30 thousand dollars in fees and expenses, we consider this experience a win as it has given us the confidence, knowledge, and information necessary to pursue future deals.

Multi-family investing is a challenging and rewarding industry. In this book, I will be sharing what I have learned with you to help you get started on your own multi-family investing journey.

I believe that anyone can become a successful multi-family housing investor with the right information, guidance, and resources. Whether you are just starting out or are an experienced investor, I am confident that you will find the information contained in this book to be both insightful and practical.

In this book, we will cover key topics such as getting started with multi-family investing, napkin underwriting, broker outreach, legal considerations, SEC regulations, property management, and much more. My goal is to provide you with a beginner's guide to multi-family housing investing that will equip you with the knowledge and tools you need to succeed.

I am proud of what my team and I have accomplished in the multi-family housing industry and I am eager to share our experiences and insights with you. Whether you are just starting out or are an experienced investor, I am confident that this book will be an invaluable resource on your journey to financial freedom.

So, let's get started!

CHAPTER 1

Introduction to Multi-Family Investing

What is Multi-Family Investing?

Multi-family investing refers to the ownership and management of multiple residential units within a single property. This type of real estate investment offers a number of benefits, including the potential for steady and consistent cash flow, a higher return on investment compared to single-family properties, and economies of scale that can result in lower operating costs.

The Value-Add Model of Multi-Family Investing

One popular approach to multi-family investing is the value-add model. This strategy involves buying a property that may require some renovations or upgrades, and then implementing these improvements to increase the rental income and property value. This can result in a higher return on investment for the investor compared to simply buying a turn-key property.

Why Invest in Multi-Family Properties?

There are several reasons why investing in multi-family properties can be a smart choice for beginner investors. Firstly, multi-family properties offer a more stable and consistent cash flow compared to single-family properties, as there are multiple tenants generating rental income. Secondly, multi-family properties can benefit from economies of scale, such as lower utility costs and a lower cost per unit for property management. Finally, multi-family properties can offer a higher return on investment compared to single-family properties, as they can provide a greater rental income and a higher appreciation in property value.

In this book, we will explore the opportunities and challenges of multi-family investing and provide a step-by-step guide for getting started with this type of real estate investment. Whether you are new to real estate investing or looking to diversify your portfolio, this book will provide the information and resources you need to succeed in the multi-family market.

The Benefits of Investing as a Limited Partner in Multi-Family Properties

Investing in multi-family properties has long been a popular choice for savvy real estate investors, and for good reason. With the ability to generate steady and consistent rental income from multiple tenants, as well as the potential for appreciation in property value, multi-family properties can provide a number of compelling benefits for investors.

As a limited partner in a multi-family investment, you have the opportunity to enjoy many of these benefits without the time and effort required to manage the property yourself. Instead, you can sit back and let the experienced professionals handle all aspects of the investment, while you enjoy a share of the profits.

Here are just a few of the key benefits of investing as a limited partner in multi-family properties:

Passive Income Stream

One of the biggest benefits of investing as a limited partner in multi-family properties is the potential for passive income. With rental income generated by multiple tenants, you can enjoy a steady and consistent flow of income without having to actively manage the property yourself. This can provide a valuable source of income, particularly if you are retired or looking for a more passive investment option.

Diversification of Investment Portfolio

Another key benefit of investing as a limited partner in multi-family properties is the ability to diversify your investment portfolio. Real estate investments offer a different type of return compared to stocks and bonds, making them a valuable addition to any portfolio. By investing in multi-family properties as a limited partner, you can take advantage of the potential for steady rental income and appreciation in property value, helping to diversify your portfolio and reduce risk.

Expert Management

When you invest as a limited partner in multi-family properties, you can take advantage of the expertise of experienced property managers. These professionals have the knowledge and experience to handle all aspects of the investment, from finding and acquiring properties, to managing and maintaining them. By outsourcing the management of your investment, you can free up your time and focus on other things, while still enjoying the benefits of multi-family investing.

Lower Risk

Investing in multi-family properties can also provide a lower level of risk compared to other types of real estate investments. With multiple tenants generating rental income, you are less dependent on a single tenant to pay the bills. Additionally, multi-family properties can benefit from economies of scale, such as lower utility costs and a lower cost per unit for property management, helping to reduce operating costs and increase profitability.

Our team, Condor Multifamily Housing Solutions, specializes in providing limited partnership investment opportunities in multi-family properties. With our expert management team and a focus on value-add investments, we offer a unique opportunity for investors to enjoy the benefits of multi-family investing without the time and effort required to manage the property themselves.

Whether you are looking for a passive income stream, a way to diversify your investment portfolio, or a lower risk investment option, investing as a limited partner in multi-family properties offers a number of compelling benefits. So why wait? Take control of your financial future and start building a more secure and profitable investment portfolio with Condor today!

The Best way as of the publication of this book to partner with us is by being part of our Facebook Community. To Join simply go to www.facebook.com/groups/thegrowgiver/

OTHER HELPFUL LINKS FOLLOW THE QR CODES BELOW:

https://condormfh.com/

https://thegrowgiver.com/

https://www.youtube.com/@thegrowgiver/

CHAPTER 2:

Getting Started with Multi-Family Investing

In this chapter, we will explore the first steps to take in getting started with multi-family investing. Understanding the value-add model is key to developing a successful investment strategy, and we will go over the key elements of this model. Additionally, we will discuss the importance of creating a strategic investment plan and assessing your finances and investment goals before moving forward with any investment.

A. Understanding the Value-Add Model

The value-add model is a popular approach in multi-family investing, where the goal is to purchase a property that has the potential for significant upgrades and improvements. These upgrades and improvements can increase the property's value and generate higher rental income, leading to higher returns for the investor. When evaluating investment opportunities, it is important to consider the potential for value-add and determine if the investment fits within your investment strategy.

B. Creating a Strategic Investment Plan

Before investing in any property, it is important to have a clear understanding of your investment goals and objectives. This will help you develop a strategic investment plan that will guide your decision-making process and ensure that you are on track to meet your goals. Your investment plan should consider factors such as your financial resources, the type of properties you are interested in investing in, and your timeline for investing.

C. Assessing Your Finances and Investment Goals

In order to successfully invest in multi-family properties, it is important to assess your finances and determine what you can afford. This will help you set realistic investment goals and ensure that you have the financial resources to make your investment. Additionally, it is important to consider the amount of time and resources you are willing to devote to managing your investment.

When getting started with multi-family investing, it is important to have a clear understanding of the value-add model, develop a strategic investment plan, and assess your finances and investment goals. By taking these steps, you can position yourself for success in this exciting and potentially lucrative area of real estate investing.

In the next chapter, we will delve into the topic of napkin underwriting, a key tool for evaluating investment opportunities in multi-family real estate.

CHAPTER 3:

Understanding the Basics of Napkin Underwriting

A. Understanding the Basics of Underwriting

Underwriting is the process of evaluating an investment opportunity to determine its potential for profitability. It is an essential step in making informed investment decisions, particularly in multi-family real estate investing.

B. Key Factors to Consider When Underwriting a Multi-Family Property

When underwriting a multi-family property, there are several key factors to consider, including the number of units, average rent, current occupancy rate, and yearly expenses. These factors will help you estimate the potential rental income and determine the Net Operating Income (NOI).

C. How to Use Napkin Underwriting to Evaluate Investment Opportunities

Napkin underwriting is a quick and easy method of evaluating investment opportunities in multi-family real estate. The formula used in napkin underwriting includes the following steps:

Find Potential: Multiply the number of units by the average rent and then multiply by 12 to estimate the potential rental income if the property were 100% occupied.

Gross Rental Income: Multiply the potential rental income by the current occupancy rate percentage to estimate the Gross Base Rental Income.

Net Operating Income: Multiply the Gross Base Rental Income by 50% to estimate the yearly expenses and subtract these expenses from the Gross Base Rental Income to determine the NOI.

Max Allowable Offer: Divide the NOI by the market cap rate to determine the maximum reasonable offer for the property.

By using napkin underwriting, you can quickly and easily evaluate the potential of a multi-family investment opportunity. This information can help you make informed investment decisions and position yourself for success in multi-family real estate investing.

In the next chapter, we will explore broker outreach for lead generation, a critical component of a successful multi-family investment strategy.

The Formula:

Step 1 Find Potential
# of units (times) avg. rents (times) 12 = potential if 100% occupied

Step 2 Gross Rental Income
potential (times) current occupancy = Gross Base Rental Income

Step 3 Net Operating Income
Gross Base Rental Income (times) .5 (Estimated Expenses) = NOI

Step 4 Max Allowable Offer
NOI Net Operating Income (divided by) cap rate = Max Allowable Offer (MAX REASONABLE OFFER)

Example:

Whisper Price: 12m, # of units 100, Current Occupancy 70%, Asset Class B, Avg. Rents $1200/mo, Cap Rate 4.65

Step 1
100 x 1200 = 120,000

120,000 x 12 = 1.44m

Step 2

1.44m x 70% = 1,008,000

Step 3
1,008,000 x .5 = 504,000 = NOI

Step 4
504,000 / 4.65 = 10,838,707.68 - 10.8m

CHAPTER 4:

Broker Outreach for Lead Generation

Investing in multi-family real estate can be a highly profitable venture. But to maximize your chances of success, you need to find the right properties to invest in. This is where brokers come in. In this chapter, we will explore the role of brokers in multi-family investing, how to find and connect with the right brokers, and strategies for maximizing your lead generation efforts.

A. Understanding the Role of Brokers in Multi-Family Investing

Brokers play a critical role in the multi-family real estate market. They are the intermediaries between buyers and sellers and have a wealth of knowledge about the properties and markets in which they work. They are the gatekeepers to the best investment opportunities and have the expertise and contacts to help you find the properties that meet your investment criteria.

Brokers can help you save time and money by conducting market research and presenting you with a shortlist of properties that fit your investment criteria. They can also help you negotiate the best deal, by leveraging their knowledge of the market and their relationships with other brokers, owners, and buyers. Additionally, brokers can provide valuable advice and guidance on legal, financial, and market-related issues.

B. How to Find and Connect with the Right Brokers

The first step in finding the right broker is to identify the market in which you are interested in investing. You can start by searching for brokers in the area by visiting websites such as loopnet.com. From the site, you can find the drop-down sandwich menu in the upper-left-hand corner of the screen, select "Find a

Broker," and then enter the market you are interested in.

Once you have identified the brokers in the market, you can further filter your search by selecting "Multifamily" from the Property Type Expertise drop-down menu and then pressing the red "Search" button on the bottom right-hand side of the screen. This will ensure that you are only seeing brokers who specialize in multi-family properties.

To ensure that your calls are targeted and have a high success rate, you should also look for brokers who identify their specialty as "Multi-family" in their profile description. This will help you to avoid brokers who may not be as experienced in this type of investment.

Finally, you should call the brokers. If they provide both an office and cell number, it is best to call the cell number as it will give you a better chance of talking directly to the broker and avoiding a gatekeeper like an office receptionist.

C. Strategies for Maximizing Your Lead Generation Efforts

When reaching out to brokers, it is important to have a clear understanding of the type of multi-family asset you are looking for. You should know the asset class, unit mix, preferred area of town, desired age of the asset, and be familiar with industry terms. This will enable you to effectively communicate with brokers and maximize your chances of finding the right investment opportunity.

Additionally, it is important to have a strong and professional demeanor when calling brokers. You should have a clear and concise script that introduces yourself, explains your investment criteria, and asks if they can help or refer you to someone who can. Being well-prepared and confident will make a positive impression and increase the likelihood that brokers will take you seriously and provide you with valuable leads.

In conclusion, broker outreach is a critical part of multi-family investing. By understanding the role of brokers, finding the right brokers, and implementing effective lead generation strategies, you can increase your chances of finding the right properties and making profitable investments. By following these steps, you will be well on your way to achieving

CHAPTER 5:

Once You've Found a Potential Deal

A. The Covert Walk Through

As a real estate investor, one of the most important steps in finding a potential deal is to conduct a thorough investigation of the property. The covert walk through is a valuable tool that we use to gather information about the property and its condition. The purpose of a covert walk through is to assess the condition of the property, determine its potential value, and gauge the competence of the current management and maintenance.

The covert walk through is a simple yet effective process where a representative from the investment team visits the property, typically posing as a potential tenant. During the covert walk through, the representative takes a close look at the property, assesses its condition, and speaks with the property management staff to gather information about the property. This can help provide a rough idea of the condition and identify any issues that may need to be addressed before making an investment decision.

One of the benefits of conducting a covert walk through is that it allows the investor to gather information about the property without arousing suspicion. Since the representative is posing as a potential tenant, the property management staff is unlikely to be defensive or guarded about sharing information about the property. Additionally, the covert walk through provides the opportunity to speak with tenants and get their opinions and feedback on the property, which can provide valuable insights into the property's condition and its potential as an investment opportunity.

It is important to note that while the covert walk through is a useful tool, it is not a substitute for a thorough due diligence process. The covert walk through should be used to gather information about the property, but it is not a comprehensive assessment of the property. To thoroughly evaluate a potential investment, the investor should conduct a complete due diligence process that includes a full review of the property's financials, a title search, and an assessment of the property's physical condition.

B. Submitting an LOI

Once the covert walk through has been conducted and the investor has determined that the property is a good investment opportunity, the next step is to submit a Letter of Intent (LOI). An LOI is a document that demonstrates the investor's intent to purchase the property and provides a preliminary outline of the terms and conditions of the proposed purchase.

The LOI typically includes information about the purchase price, the financing structure, the length of the due diligence period, and the closing date. The LOI also includes any contingencies that the investor may have, such as obtaining financing or conducting a thorough due diligence process. The purpose of the LOI is to communicate the investor's interest in the property and provide the seller with a preliminary understanding of the terms of the proposed purchase.

In most cases, the LOI is not a binding agreement, but rather a non-binding statement of the investor's intent to purchase the property. However, it is important to remember that the LOI can set the tone for the negotiations and can impact the final agreement. Therefore, it is important to ensure that the LOI accurately reflects the investor's intentions and includes all relevant information.

C. Negotiating the LOI

Once the LOI has been submitted, the next step is to negotiate the terms of the agreement. The negotiation process is an important step in the purchase of a property, as it determines the final terms and conditions of the agreement. Negotiations typically involve discussions about the purchase price, financing structure, due diligence period, and closing date.

The negotiation process is an opportunity for both the buyer and the seller to come to a mutually agreed upon terms for the sale of the property. During this process, it is important for both parties to be transparent about their expectations and for the buyer to clearly communicate any concerns or questions about the property. This is where the LOI comes into play, as it serves as a preliminary agreement between the buyer and the seller, outlining the terms and conditions of the sale.

The LOI is a crucial step in the process because it helps both parties to establish a clear understanding of the terms of the sale, prior to entering into a more formal agreement. It is important to note that the LOI is not a binding agreement, but it does provide a framework for the negotiation process and sets the tone for a productive and successful negotiation.

The negotiation process can involve a number of important factors, including the purchase price, the amount of financing to be provided by the seller, the length of the due diligence period, and the closing date. It is important for the buyer to consider these factors carefully and to clearly communicate their needs and concerns to the seller during the negotiation process.

One of the most important aspects of the negotiation process is determining the purchase price of the property. This can be a complex process and will often require input from real estate professionals, such as appraisers and brokers, to help determine the fair market value of the property. The buyer should also consider the costs associated with buying and owning the property, such as taxes, insurance, and maintenance expenses, when determining the purchase price.

In addition to the purchase price, the seller may also agree to provide financing to the buyer in order to facilitate the sale of the property. This can be an attractive option for the buyer, as it allows them to secure the property without having to come up with the full purchase price upfront. However, it is important for the buyer to carefully consider the terms of any financing offered by the seller, such as the interest rate, the length of the loan, and the repayment schedule.

Another important aspect of the negotiation process is the length of the due diligence period. The due diligence period is the time between the signing of the PSA and the close of escrow, during which the buyer has the opportunity to conduct a thorough investigation of the property and determine if it meets their expectations and needs. This period is critical for the buyer, as it allows them to gather information about the property and to assess any potential risks or issues before committing to the sale.

Finally, the closing date is an important aspect of the negotiation process. This is the date on which the sale of the property will be finalized and the ownership will transfer from the seller to the buyer. The closing date should be agreed upon by both parties and should allow enough time for the buyer to complete their due diligence and for any financing to be arranged.

In conclusion, the negotiation process is an essential part of the real estate transaction and requires careful consideration of a number of important factors. The LOI serves as a preliminary agreement between the buyer and the seller and provides a framework for the negotiation process. The buyer should carefully consider the purchase price, any financing offered by the seller, the length of the due diligence period, and the closing date, in order to ensure a successful and productive negotiation. A good attorney can be an invaluable resource in the negotiation process, as they can help to protect the buyer's interests and ensure that the terms of the sale are fair and favorable for both parties.

CHAPTER 6:

The Importance of an Attorney for Purchase and Sales Agreements

A. Overview of the Role of an Attorney in Real Estate Transactions

An attorney plays a critical role in real estate transactions, including multi-family investments. They are responsible for reviewing and negotiating purchase and sales agreements (PSA) and ensuring that the transaction is carried out in compliance with the law. Attorneys also provide legal guidance and representation to protect the interests of their clients.

B. Understanding the Legal Considerations in Multi-Family Transactions

Multi-family transactions involve a complex array of legal considerations, including zoning laws, tax laws, and regulations related to ownership and operation of multi-family properties. It is essential to have an attorney who is knowledgeable about these legal issues and can advise you on the best course of action.

The PSA is a crucial document in any real estate transaction, and it is essential that it is reviewed and negotiated by an attorney. An attorney can ensure that the PSA is legally binding and enforceable and that it accurately reflects the terms and conditions agreed upon by both parties. They can also identify potential risks and issues and work with the parties to resolve them.

C. How an Attorney Can Protect Your Interests and Ensure a Successful Transaction

Having an attorney involved in your multi-family transaction can help protect your interests and ensure a successful outcome. They can provide legal representation during negotiations, advise on contract terms, and ensure that all necessary due diligence is carried out. Additionally, an attorney can provide advice on any legal issues that arise during the transaction and represent you in court if necessary.

In conclusion, it is essential to have an attorney involved in your multi-family investment transactions. They bring valuable expertise and legal knowledge to the table and can help you navigate the complex legal landscape associated with multi-family investing. With their help, you can be confident that your transactions will be handled efficiently, legally, and successfully.

As we learned from our own experience in our most recent deal, having an attorney who was knowledgeable and experienced in multi-family transactions was essential. Their assistance in negotiating the PSA and guiding us through the due diligence process was invaluable, and we would not have been able to complete that aspect of the transaction without them.

CHAPTER 7:
THE IMPORTANCE OF AN ATTORNEY FOR PURCHASE AND SALES AGREEMENTS

A. Overview of SEC Regulations for Real Estate Investment

The Securities and Exchange Commission (SEC) regulates the sale of securities in the United States. When it comes to real estate investment, the SEC has specific regulations that must be followed to ensure that investors are protected and that the sale of securities is done in a fair and transparent manner.

One of the main regulations that real estate investors must comply with is Regulation D, which provides an exemption from the registration requirements of the Securities Act of 1933. This regulation allows companies to raise capital from accredited investors through private placement offerings.

B. The Importance of Staying in Compliance with SEC Regulations

Staying in compliance with SEC regulations is important for several reasons. First, it protects investors by ensuring that the sale of securities is done in a fair and transparent manner. This helps to prevent fraud and other illegal activities in the real estate investment industry.

Second, being in compliance with SEC regulations is a legal requirement. If a company does not comply with these regulations, it may face legal consequences, including fines and penalties.

Finally, being in compliance with SEC regulations helps to maintain the integrity of the real estate investment industry. This can lead to increased investor confidence, which can result in more capital being available for real estate investment.

C. How an Attorney Can Help Ensure Compliance with SEC Regulations

An attorney who is experienced in SEC regulations can help ensure that a real estate investment company is in compliance with these regulations. This can include reviewing offering documents, helping to structure the offering, and providing ongoing compliance support.

An attorney can also help a real estate investment company understand the differences between the various Regulation D offerings, such as the differences between a 506(b) and a 506(c). They can provide guidance on which type of offering is best for the company, based on its specific circumstances and goals.

Having an attorney who is knowledgeable about SEC regulations can also help to minimize the risk of legal consequences and can help to ensure that the offering is conducted in a compliant and efficient manner.

In conclusion, compliance with SEC regulations is important for protecting investors, meeting legal requirements, and maintaining the integrity of the real estate investment industry. An attorney who is experienced in these regulations can help ensure that a real estate investment company is in compliance and can provide guidance and support throughout the offering process.

CHAPTER 8:

The Importance of Partnering with a Good Property Manager or Property Management Company

A. They can do a detailed walk through with you helping you identify problems

One of the benefits of partnering with a good property manager or property management company is that they can help you with a detailed walk-through of the property. This is an opportunity to identify any problems or issues that may arise in the future, allowing you to proactively address them and reduce the risk of unexpected costs. With their expertise, they can help you identify areas that need improvement and provide you with recommendations for how to address these issues.

B. They can help you find and achieve Value add goals

Another benefit of working with a property manager is that they can help you achieve your value-add goals. They have the experience and knowledge to help you identify areas that can be improved to increase the value of the property, such as updating the common areas, improving energy efficiency, or adding new amenities. With their help, you can ensure that your investments are optimized for maximum return.

C. They have the experience and expertise to handle day-to-day operations and maintenance

Finally, a good property manager or property management company can help you handle day-to-day operations and maintenance. They have the expertise to ensure that the property is well-maintained and that the tenants are satisfied. This includes handling issues like repairs, rent collection, and lease enforcement, which can be time-consuming and complex. By partnering with a property manager, you can save time and energy and focus on growing your investment portfolio.

In conclusion, partnering with a good property manager or property management company is essential for ensuring the success of your real estate investments. They can help you identify problems, achieve value-add goals, and handle day-to-day operations and maintenance, all while freeing up your time and resources to focus on other areas of your business.

CHAPTER 9:

Conclusion

A. Recap of Key Takeaways

Multi-family investing can be a lucrative and rewarding investment opportunity, especially for those who are looking to enter the real estate market as a limited partner. This book provided an overview of the key considerations and steps involved in multi-family investing, from understanding the value-add model and creating a strategic investment plan, to identifying investment opportunities and executing a successful transaction.

A key takeaway from this book is the importance of having a clear understanding of your financial goals and assessing your finances before embarking on any investment. Napkin underwriting is a valuable tool for evaluating investment opportunities and understanding the key factors that contribute to the success of a multi-family property.

Another key takeaway is the importance of partnering with a good broker for lead generation, an attorney for legal guidance, and a property manager or management company for day-to-day operations and maintenance. These professionals can help ensure a successful transaction and protect your interests throughout the investment process.

In addition, this book highlighted the importance of compliance with SEC regulations, as well as the role of an attorney in ensuring compliance and protecting your interests in real estate transactions.

Overall, multi-family investing requires careful planning and execution, but with the right approach, it can be a profitable and long-term investment opportunity. It is essential to conduct thorough research, understand your financial goals and limitations, and seek guidance from experienced professionals when necessary.

B. Final Thoughts on Multi-Family Investing for Beginners

In conclusion, multi-family investing can provide investors with significant benefits and opportunities for growth, but it is important to approach it with caution, diligence, and a well-informed understanding of the market and its dynamics. By following the steps outlined in this book, you can increase your chances of success and build a profitable and sustainable investment portfolio in multi-family real estate.

APPENDIX 1

MULTIFAMILY TERMINOLOGY

30/30/30 = 30 Days Due Diligence/ 30 Days to raise financing/ 30 Days for Extension

Standard Carve Outs =. Environmental Surveys, other surveys, Title Searches, and other pre-purchase due diligence items.

Going Hard = This is a term to refer to earnest money or a portion of earnest money being nonrefundable.

EM or EMD = Earnest Money Deposit. Normally 1-2% down with a portion "going hard" or becoming nonrefundable after Due Diligence.

OM = Offering Memorandum - This is a basic overview and business plan of the property and projected returns provided by the seller or broker.

IRR = Internal Rate of Return-The annual rate of growth that an investment is expected to generate.

ARR = Annual Rate of Return- A process for determining investment returns on an annual basis.

DSCR Loan = Debt Service to Credit Ratio - This is a typical business type loan. A measure of a company's available cash flow to pay current debt obligations. Does a company have enough income to pay its debts? Net operating income÷Total debt service

MAO = Maximum Allowable Offer-for multifamily, it is the maximum price point you can offer and still profit.

RUBS = A system for distributing the utilities among the residence of the housing complex

LOI = Letter of Intent (Offer)- A serious proposal to purchase a property or asset.

KP = Key Principle - This is a subject knowledge expert who has real world experience and a reputation that lends credibility to an individual deal.

Rent Roll = The current rent rates per occupied unit and lease information including length of lease and other information about the units.

PROFORMA = Is the potential value of the property based upon raising rents and other income producing value adds - Note: Sellers and brokers may try to sell based upon the potential, don't pay for the work you're going to do. The work you do to increase the value of the property should be your reward for that labor.

NOI = Net Operating Income (Income - Expenses)

Cap Rate = Measure used to estimate and compare the rates of return on multiple commercial real estate properties. Calculated by NOI divided by Purchase Price

Stabilization Period = The estimated time it will take to increase the rents to market value

P&L = Profit and Loss Statement- A financial statement that summarizes the revenues, costs and expenses during a specified time period (eg- quarterly, annually, etc)

T12 = A document showing the itemized and total net profit of the asset over the most recent 12 month period.

Fund = Is a pool of investors

Private Money = Each lender will have their own loan docs.

Reg D = Regulation D (Reg D) is the U.S. Securities and Exchange Commission (SEC) regulation pertaining to private placement exemptions. It does not relate to bank account restrictions issued by the Federal Reserve Board. Securities offerings are beneficial for businesses or individuals that meet the requirements because they can be financed quicker and at a lower cost than with a public offering. It's usually used by smaller companies. However, other state and federal regulations remain in place.

506B = Investors in fund are not accredited investors, but associates/friends/ ect. (35 max allowed) You cannot solicit investors with this fund as you must have a prior relationship with each investor.

506C = Investors in fund must be Accredited investors.

Accredited Investor = A single investor who has earned at least $200K (or $300K together with a spouse) in each of the two prior years and reasonably expects the same in the current year OR who has a net worth of $1M excluding the value of their primary residence.

WHISPER PRICE = This is pricing information the broker may share to let a potential buyer know where the offers on a property are trending. This can help you as a buyer to bring a competitive offer.

OCCUPANCY RATE = The percentage of total units that are currently rented out.

REG CF = Regulation Crowd Fund - The cap for this is 5 Million raised - the assets cannot be valued for more than 25 million

PPM = Private Placement Memorandum - The securities document that explains to the investors what kind of returns they will receive.

Securities Attorney - The attorney who will help you not go to jail when raising capital for your deals. They will advise on which Reg D chapter to use for a given asset.

3rd Party Clearing House = They will charge 2-6%, they will be found by your Securities Attorney. They can drive investors to your deals but they will charge you more.

SUPER FUND or (Fund of Funds) = It raises capital from institutional investors such as pensions, sovereign wealth funds, endowments, and high-net-worth individuals, and it invests that capital in specific PE firms. Both the Major Fund manager and the smaller fund managers make money by charging a percentage of the funds raised. In addition they get equity in the deals funded based on their role even if they do not invest a penny of their own money.

CAPEX = Capital expenditure- improvements to a fixed asset that will increase the value or useful life of the investment.

VALUE ADD = An investment in an asset with existing cash flow (and value) that can be increased by raising occupancy, rents, and/or added amenities (laundry, parking, pet fees etc.)

Pref eq = Preferred Equity, Preferred equity holders receive a higher priority in terms of return on investment compared to common equity holders, but typically do not have the same level of control or voting rights as common equity holders. Preferred equity can be a useful tool for real estate investors looking to raise capital for a specific project or property, and can offer a higher degree of security compared to other types of equity investments.

APPENDIX 2

Sample Script for Talking with Brokers:

[Introduction]

Hi, my name is [Your Name] and I am interested in exploring opportunities in the multi-family real estate market. I came across your profile and I was impressed with your experience and expertise in this field. I would love the opportunity to learn more about what you do and see how I can potentially work with you.

[Building a Connection]

I would love to hear more about your experience in the multi-family real estate market, and how you approach lead generation and deal sourcing. Can you tell me a little bit about your process and what sets you apart from other brokers in the industry?

[Gaining Insights]

I am specifically interested in the value-add model, and I would love to learn more about the types of properties you have worked on and the strategies you have used to maximize returns for your clients. Can you share any success stories or lessons you have learned along the way?

[Defining Your Investment Goals]

I am looking to invest in multi-family properties that provide a stable and consistent return on investment, with a focus on long-term value creation. I am open to various deal structures, but I would like to understand the key factors you consider when evaluating opportunities, and how you help your clients identify properties that match their investment goals.

[Exploring Potential Opportunities]

I would also love to hear about any current or upcoming opportunities you may have, and how I can potentially get involved. I understand that multi-family investments can be complex, but I am eager to learn and I believe that with the right guidance and support, I can make informed decisions that align with my investment goals.

[Closing Thoughts]

Thank you for taking the time to speak with me today, I truly appreciate your insights and guidance. I am excited about the potential for a long-term partnership, and I look forward to exploring opportunities together. Please let me know if there is anything else I can do to support your efforts, and I look forward to hearing from you soon.

APPENDIX 3

The LOI or Letter of Intent is very important and must be professional.

The LOI should include:
1. Your Company Logo
   a. Your Company Name
   b. Your Name
   c. Your contact information
2. The Purchase Price (Offer Price)
3. Your Financing Structure - How you are going to secure the needed funds
4. Earnest Money
   a. Refundable/non-refundanble
   b. Contingencies
5. Timing - how long you will need to raise the needed funds, do due diligence, ect.
6. Who pays what closing costs
7. Any other important terms or contingencies

SAMPLE

January 1, 20XX

Name of Complex   ****

123 S MAIN ST,

12345

Dear Seller/Broker,

After review of the information provided, YOUR COMPANY NAME and/or its assignee hereby submit this Letter of Intent (this "Letter") to the current owner ("Seller"), care of the addressee hereof, to acquire the above-referenced property (the "Properties") on the following terms and conditions:

PURCHASE PRICE:

FINANCING:

DEPOSIT TO ESCROW:

DUE DILIGENCE: # of Days

CLOSING: # of Days or Date

CLOSING COST:

REPRESENTATIONS

& WARRANTIES:

COMMISSION: Seller will be responsible for commission to broker

TITLE: TBD

TRANSACTION CONTINGENCIES:

PURCHASER:

ACKNOWLEDGED AND AGREED TO BY SELLER:

_____,DATE

_____, DATE

Name: Name:

Title: Title:

Company Name: